Jarome Iginla

Also by Nicole Mortillaro in the Lorimer Recordbooks series:
Something to Prove: The story of hockey tough guy Bobby Clarke

Jarome Iginla

How the NHL's first black captain gives back

Nicole Mortillaro

James Lorimer & Company Ltd., Publishers
Toronto

James Lorimer & Company Ltd., Publishers acknowledges the support of the
Ontario Arts Council. We acknowledge the financial support of the Government
of Canada through the Canada Book Fund for our publishing activities. We
acknowledge the support of the Canada Council for the Arts for our publishing
program. We acknowledge the Government of Ontario through the Ontario
Media Development Corporation's Ontario Book Initiative.

The Canada Council | Le Conseil des Arts
for the Arts | du Canada

ONTARIO ARTS COUNCIL
CONSEIL DES ARTS DE L'ONTARIO

Library and Archives Canada Cataloguing in Publication

Mortillaro, Nicole,
    Jarome Iginla : how the NHL's first Black captain gives back / Nicole Mortillaro.

(Recordbooks)
Issued also in an electronic format.
ISBN 978-1-55277-542-4 (bound).—ISBN 978-1-55277-541-7 (pbk.)

1. Iginla, Jarome, 1977—Juvenile literature. 2. Black Canadian hockey
players—Biography—Juvenile literature. I. Title. II. Series: Record books

GV848.5.I35M67 2010   j796.962092   C2010-904065-1

James Lorimer & Company Ltd., Publishers   Distributed in the United
317 Adelaide Street West,   States by:
Suite #1002   Orca Book Publishers
Toronto, ON, Canada   P.O. Box 468
M5V 1P9   Custer, WA USA
www.lorimer.ca   98240-0468

Printed and bound in Canada.
Manufactured by Printcrafters in Winnipeg, Manitoba, Canada in August 2010.
Job # 27287

To Sara, my family, and my tireless editor, Carrie

Contents

Prologue

The Stanley Cup.

It was within reach. It was so close. As captain of the Calgary Flames, Jarome Iginla was ready to take it. It was unlike him to seem so hungry for something. His normally generous nature had taken a backseat to his drive for the Cup. Like every player on his team, Jarome had been dreaming of it from his earliest days on ice. And here he was — part of the 2004 run to the National Hockey League's top prize.

The arena was loud. Fans cheered as the anthem ended. But the players from both teams — the Calgary Flames and the Tampa Bay Lightning — were focused. They knew they had to play their hardest and their best.

The series had been a tight one. The teams seemed evenly matched. They went back and forth within each game. But now it was a game that both teams desperately wanted to win. The series was tied at two apiece heading into this fifth game. The winner would command a 3–2 lead in the series. They would be just one game away from hoisting the coveted trophy. And Jarome wanted this. Both teams desperately wanted to win.

The Flames started the game off scoring when Toni Lydman scored off a tip-in. But the Lightning were still very much in the series. They wouldn't give up. They tied it up late in the first period. It was obvious that this was going to be another tight game.

Jarome was his team's leader. The polite and soft-spoken young man knew how to lead by example. In the second period, after a flurry around Tampa Bay's goalie, Nikolai Khabibulin, he skated in to his player's defense. Some Lightning players had started to push and shove. He wasn't going to get pushed around, and he wasn't about to let his teammates be pushed around either.

And then, late in the second period, Jarome did what he does best.

There were just over four minutes left in the second. Jarome flew down the right wing, the puck on his stick. For a brief moment, he looked to see who might be coming down centre ice to take the shot from the point. But there was nobody in position. It was obvious that Khabibulin was ready for Jarome to pass off the puck.

But Jarome decided to take the shot himself. He fired it hard and in it went. He had tied the game!

"Well," said CBC *Hockey Night in Canada* broadcaster Harry Neale. "How about that shot!"

Jarome celebrated with his teammates. But he knew that this wasn't over. And he was right. It would be another hard-fought game as it headed into overtime.

1 A Star is Born

On July 1, 1977, families across the country celebrated Canada Day. They enjoyed the festivities in their towns and cities. There were balloons and picnics and candy, and, of course, fireworks.

But in Edmonton, Alberta, Susan and Elvis Iginla skipped the celebrations of their adopted country — and for good reason. They were awaiting the arrival of their first child. When Jarome Arthur-Leigh Adekunle Tig Junior Elvis Iginla arrived that day, they breathed a sigh of relief.

Jarome's father emigrated from Nigeria to Canada when he was just nineteen. He changed his name from Adekunle to Elvis, because most people had trouble pronouncing his African name. Young and determined, Elvis put himself through law school at the University of Alberta, and began practising law. Jarome's mother, Susan was originally from Medford, Oregon. She worked as a massage therapist and music teacher. Just two years after Jarome was born, Susan and Elvis separated. Jarome grew up with his mother in St. Albert, Alberta, about 75 kilometres (47 miles) northwest of Edmonton.

Like most boys, Jarome enjoyed sports. His mother would always keep him busy, whether it was baseball, tennis, or even bowling.

"I played a lot of different sports growing up," Jarome says. "It was a great way for me to vent all my energy. My mom always said I had too much energy."

It wasn't until Jarome was almost seven years old that he was introduced to hockey. The seed of playing in the NHL was planted one day after his aunt took him to an arena to watch a local game. Although his parents didn't know much about hockey, his grandfather was always willing to help him.

"My grandparents believed in the value of sport and worked really hard to help my mom get me to hockey." Jarome says.

But as much as Jarome enjoyed hockey, he was very aware of the difference between him and almost every other National Hockey League (NHL) superstar: he was of mixed race. There hadn't been many black NHLers in the game.

"Growing up, I was aware that I was

the only one [black player] on my team," he once said in an interview. "Kids used to ask me all the time what are my chances, there aren't any black players in the NHL, and I'm one of them."

Years later, in an interview with *Jet*, an American magazine for blacks, he said, "When I started playing and watching hockey as a seven-year-old, I was aware of it. Also kids would say, when I [told them I] wanted to be in the NHL, that there are not very many black players in the NHL. So I really was aware of it . . . but I wanted to be in the NHL and be like my idols."

Another time he noted, "It made me feel good to see other [black] players who were making it in the NHL. After that, I never worried about what the odds were. I knew it was possible."

Jarome enrolled in a minor hockey program. Like his hockey idol, Grant Fuhr, Jarome wanted to be goalie. But his

Oilers in the 80s

When Jarome was growing up in the 1980s, the Edmonton Oilers were a strong team. With stars like goalie Grant Fuhr, defenseman Paul Coffey, and forwards Mark Messier and The Great One himself, Wayne Gretzky, the team won four Stanley Cups between 1984 and 1987. Grant Fuhr was key to the team's success. He was born in Spruce Grove, Alberta, about 20 kilometres (12 miles) from Jarome's first home in St. Albert. Fuhr was also of mixed race. By the end of his time with the Oilers, Fuhr had played a record 4,304 minutes and led his team to five Stanley Cups. He won the Vezina Trophy for his goaltending and was even the runner-up for the Hart Trophy, tying with teammate Wayne Gretzky.

time in goal didn't last long. Two years later, he moved to right wing, playing in the St. Albert Minor Hockey Association. He played his entire minor hockey career there with the Bantam AAA Sabres and then the Midget AAA Raiders. In his final year with the Raiders, as an underage player, he scored 87 goals and led the league in scoring.

Jarome's mother worked hard to keep him in sports. His grandfather also helped by driving him to practices — even if they were for other sports. Jarome was quite the all-around athlete. Not only was he becoming an extremely talented hockey player, he was also a baseball player. In the early 1990s, he earned the starting position as catcher for the Canadian junior baseball team.

Jarome started his junior hockey career when he was sixteen years old. He played for the Kamloops Blazers of the Western Hockey League (WHL) in 1993–94. That season, he had 6 goals and 23 assists for 29 points in 48 games. He obviously had a gift for the sport.

Jarome started playing for the Kamloops Blazers in 1993–1994.

The following season, he tallied 33 goals and 37 assists in 77 games. Jarome was a well-rounded player. He had the physical presence on the ice. He also had a scoring touch and made his plays count. And he wasn't an "ugly" player. After his team's Memorial Cup victory in 1994–95 he was awarded the George Parsons Trophy for the most sportsmanlike conduct. In all, by the end of his junior career with the Blazers, Jarome earned 246 points and helped carry his team to two Memorial Cups.

The Memorial Cup

The Memorial Cup is a major hockey award in Canada. The award was donated by the Ontario Hockey Association in 1919. It marks the remembrance of soldiers who died in WWI. Teams from the Canadian Hockey League, which consists of the Quebec Major Junior League, Western Hockey League, and the Ontario Hockey League compete for the trophy each year.

Jarome's incredible performances with the Blazers didn't go unnoticed. He was one of the most talented players in the WHL. And, like most hockey players, he had one dream. He wanted to make it to the National Hockey League. It didn't matter if people thought he looked different from other NHL players.

2 Drafted!

Jarome proved that he had the talent to play with the best in the junior league. It came as no surprise to anyone that he had his sights set on a future in the NHL. He continued to play his best, with the hope that it would carry him forward.

As luck would have it, the 1995 NHL Entry Draft was held in his hometown of Edmonton. Imagine what it would feel like to be drafted into the NHL right at home!

Jarome was still living with his mother. He knew that all his hard work — and the sacrifices of his mother and grandfather — would be worth it if he could make it into the NHL.

Jarome anxiously awaited draft day. This would be the day that he'd been dreaming of since he had first fallen in love with hockey. So many young men dreamed of this day. He knew that he was lucky to be considered in the draft.

The day was soon upon him. It was a cloudy summer day in Edmonton. But the overcast skies didn't put a damper on Jarome's spirits. Which team would draft him? It didn't really matter where he went, so long as he could play. But still, it might be nice to play close to home.

There was a lot of young talent in that year's draft. Jarome, like other players, wondered if he would go early or be left to the end.

The Winnipeg Jets

The Winnipeg Jets played in the NHL from 1979 to 1996. The team first came into being in 1971, as part of the World Hockey Association (WHA). The WHA was a rival hockey organization to the NHL and folded in 1979. The Winnipeg Jets moved to Phoenix and became the Phoenix Coyotes in 1996.

Names were called: Bryan Berard went first, to Ottawa. Then Wayne Redden to the New York Islanders. Jarome's teammate Shane Doan was drafted seventh overall by the Winnipeg Jets.

Jarome waited patiently as the names were called. Then finally, the moment he'd been waiting for:

"Jarome Iginla."

He had been drafted, in the first round, eleventh overall, by the Dallas Stars. He was elated.

But now the hard work would *really* begin.

3 "What's an Iginla?"

Young Jarome knew what it meant to work hard for what he wanted. He had done it his whole life. But being drafted by an NHL team was something else. He knew that, although they were teammates, he was pitted against other talented young men. Every one of them wanted to make the team. He had to prove that he deserved to be called up to the Stars.

And the Dallas Stars knew that, although Jarome was a good player, there was still room for improvement. Anyone who is drafted needs to learn more. Jarome showed up in Dallas at their training camp in September. He spent time practising with the team. Then he returned to British Columbia and the team in Kamloops. He worked on his skating, agility, and conditioning.

But while eighteen-year-old Jarome worked on becoming a better and stronger player, other forces were in play that would change his hockey career.

Behind closed doors, Jarome's NHL future was taking shape. The Calgary Flames were having issues with their star forward, Joe Nieuwendyk. They couldn't agree on a contract. It was obvious that the team and Nieuwendyk were not going to be able to settle their differences. But the Dallas Stars were willing to give up their top prospect, Jarome, for Nieuwendyk. On December 19, 1995, Jarome — along

Jarome after he was drafted in the 1995 NHL Entry Draft by the Dallas Stars.

with centre Corey Millen — went to Calgary.

Calgary Flames general manager Al Coates wasn't very popular for the trade. Nieuwendyk was a Calgary favourite. "We felt sure back then that he'd play in the league," Coates said about Jarome later in a newspaper article. "We hoped he'd be a good player. But to sit here today and try and tell you we were certain he'd become the horse that he is, the star that he's become, that would be presumptuous. I'd like to, believe me, but I can't."

Many people felt that Calgary was giving up far too much for an unproven player.

Superstar Flames defenseman Al MacInnis said, "I think what everyone else in the league thinks of it — not much. I don't know what Calgary was thinking. Was that the best deal on the table? Dallas didn't have to give up anything."

One newspaper even wrote: "Joe Nieuwendyk for Jarome Iginla? It stinks!" Even a newspaper in Florida boasted the headline, "What's an Iginla? The Flames know."

Jarome said at the time, "I guess maybe

it's a little pressure. But it's not a bad thing because it helps me work harder. It's exciting, too, because it means they [the Calgary Flames] have confidence in you."

It would be up to Jarome to show his critics what an Iginla was.

4 Best of the Best

Jarome had been in training camp for the World Juniors when he was traded to Calgary. The World Junior Championship showcased the best in junior hockey. That year, the tournament took place in Boston, Massachusetts.

By this time, it was evident that Jarome belonged with the elite in the junior category. But he didn't let it go to his head. He was modest and grateful to be representing his country.

Team Canada and the Juniors

The World Junior Championships is an international hockey event organized by the International Ice Hockey Federation for players under twenty years old. Teams from around the world send their very best young men to compete for the title. The first year of the championship was 1977. The Soviet Union (now commonly referred to as the Russian team) won the first seven of ten titles. But now Canada leads with the most wins at fifteen.

Team Canada had captured the gold in 1993, 1994, and 1995. There was great pressure on this team to bring home the gold again. Jarome was up to the challenge. In their 6–1 win over the United States, Jarome got two assists. Then, in the second game, he scored one goal and one assist against Finland.

Although some said the competition in

the Juniors wasn't as fierce as it had been in the past, the 1996 Canadian team was strong: their defense was tight. It made any offense from opposing teams nearly useless. In all eight games, the Canadians — with Jose Theodore and Marc Denis sharing the job in goal — set a record by giving up just six goals.

Jarome shone. He gave the most important performance of his career so far. On January 3, 1996, Jarome netted the winner in a close semifinal game against Team Canada's rivals, the Russians. This 4–3 win sent Canada to the gold-medal game where they would face Sweden. Could Jarome top getting the winning goal in a semifinal game?

He did. In the gold-medal game, he came out as a powerhouse. He assisted on three of the four goals in the country's 4–1 win. Canada won its fourth-straight gold in the championship, due to a hard-working team and the talent of its young stars.

In that tournament, Jarome earned 12 points, and was named the best forward.

Afterwards, Jarome went back to preparing for the NHL. He returned to the Kamloops Blazers a different person. At eighteen years old, he was now a young man, a World Juniors star, and an NHL first-round draft pick.

This was his third season with the Blazers, and it would be one of his best. Jarome came out blazing, getting 63 goals and 73 assists in 63 games. He had his best night in one game against the Seattle Thunderbirds when he tallied seven points! He also had 120 penalty minutes — up from a mere 33 in his first year with the team. This showed that he could be both a defensive and an offensive presence on the ice.

While playing for the Blazers, Jarome had his best season in 1995–96 when he tallied 136 points.

5 Highs and Lows

Almost immediately after the Kamloops Blazers were eliminated from the WHL playoffs, the Flames had Jarome on his way to the Stanley Cup playoffs. The afternoon after the Blazers' elimination, Jarome made his NHL debut against the Chicago Blackhawks.

On April 21, 1996, Jarome took to the ice at home in Calgary.

Chicago was leading 2–0 in the series. Being on home ice meant home advantage, and the Flames hoped to capitalize on it. Unfortunately, they lost in a high-scoring game, 7–5. But for Jarome, it was a special night: he got an assist. It was his first NHL point! Two nights later, he scored Calgary's only goal in a 2–1 loss to Chicago. Once again, Jarome was faced with personal success, rather than a greater team success. The team's loss meant that Calgary was eliminated from the playoffs. But Jarome had made his mark. In two games, he managed to earn two points — a healthy start to a professional hockey career.

The following season was, as it is with any player taking his first step in the NHL, a learning experience for Jarome.

One Calgary newspaper would refer to Jarome as "Jarome Who." But it didn't matter to him. He knew what he had to do. And he wasn't doing it for anyone else but himself.

*Jarome played in his first NHL game for the Calgary
Flames during the 1995–1996 playoffs.*

The "Battle of Alberta"

Although it was nice for Jarome to return to Alberta after playing in British Columbia, it was a bittersweet return home. As an Edmonton boy, he had grown up a loyal Oilers fan. As often happens with neighbouring professional sports teams, there was a fierce rivalry between Edmonton Oilers fans and the Calgary Flames fans to the south. Even today, when these two face off against each other it's called the "Battle of Alberta."

Iginla started his first full NHL season with a bang. He played on a line with fellow rookie Jonas Höglund and league veteran Dave Gagner, giving him the chance to learn from an older player. He knew that he couldn't slack off. He showed that he was both mentally and physically able to endure the rigours of the NHL — he was just one of three Flames who played the full 82 games of the season.

He reached 21 goals and tallied 50 points, leading all NHL rookies in 1996–97. He also made the All-Star rookie team. And that season, he finished second in voting for the Calder Memorial Trophy. This trophy goes to the NHL player judged as the "most proficient in his first year of competition." People were no longer asking, "Jarome who?"

Although Jarome had a very successful year personally, Calgary missed the play-offs. The question was, how would Jarome fare the next season? Could he keep up the pace?

It seems as though every NHL player suffers from what is referred to as a "sophomore season." This means that a player's second season isn't as great as his first. It could be due to many reasons. One reason may be that a player goes into a second season after a fairly successful one thinking that he has it made. But in order to be a good player — in order to be good at anything — you have to work at it.

Jarome did suffer from a sophomore season. In 70 games, he only scored 13 goals. But it wasn't just Jarome who suffered. The Flames as a whole had a dismal year. In the 1997–98 season, the club finished with a 26–41–15 record. Obviously, they didn't make the playoffs.

The fact that Jarome was different was never far from his mind. He once told ESPN, "What I mostly heard was 'Why are you playing hockey? There are no black players in the NHL. What are your chances?'"

But he wasn't one to give up easily. He thought back to the black heroes of the NHL. They had proven that it didn't matter if someone was black or white. If they had the talent, they could make it in the NHL.

"Those guys were really helpful in

Black NHL Heroes

Having black players break through in the NHL took a lot of time. The first black player in an NHL game was Willie O'Ree in 1958. O'Ree, from Fredericton, New Brunswick, appeared in his first game as a Boston Bruin at the Montreal Forum on January 18, 1958. Although he only played in two games that season, he returned for the 1960–61 season, scoring 4 goals and 10 assists. O'Ree was also partially blind in one eye, but chose to keep it a secret in order to play. It was thirteen years later that Mike Marson became the second black player in the NHL. Even after all those years — and even today — black players had to endure racist remarks from fans, players, and even coaches. Despite these obstacles, black players have found great success in the NHL. Grant Fuhr is considered one of the most successful goalies in the NHL. Today there are many great black players, such as Jarome, Anson Carter, Dustin Byfuglien, and P.K. Subban.

me following my dream," he once told NHL.com. "I'd be flattered if I could be someone [black kids] looked up to and see as someone that will help them follow their dream."

The pressure was on Jarome to prove that it *was* just the sophomore jinx and that his success wasn't just luck. He had to show that he belonged in the NHL.

6 Fanning the Flames

Both Jarome and the Calgary Flames knew they had to do better. And both the young man and the team knew they could do it. There was always room for improvement. It just meant more hard work. So Jarome focused even more.

During the 1998–99 season, the Calgary Flames finished with 72 points. Jarome scored 28 goals and 23 assists for 51 points, a team best. Yet, the Flames didn't have a lot of player support around its newest upstart. Even though they had improved, they missed the playoffs again.

The next season was a tough one for Jarome. He ended up in one of the worst slumps of his career during the first half of the season. He picked up the pace during the second half. He scored 29 goals and 34 assists for 63 points. It was obvious that every year in the NHL was making him a better player. This was something the Flames had hoped to see from him. He was determined and focused. Each night he showed up ready to give it his all. Hockey was important to him, but so was doing his best. It was a value that had been passed on to him by his family. Hard work was important. Hard work ended in results.

He once told a magazine, "Every day, I realize how blessed I've been in my life. From the time I was seven years old, I wanted to play in the NHL, and to this day, it's awesome, it's fun, and I realize it's not going to last forever."

In the next season, he tried to do even better. The 2000–01 season was very productive for Jarome. In 77 games, he had 31 goals and 40 assists for a career high of 71 points. Jarome was a legitimate hockey star.

But he wasn't done. Jarome had become a positive role model for young black players. He wanted to encourage *all* children to play sports. Black, white, Asian, Aboriginal — their backgrounds didn't matter. Jarome wanted children to be able to pick up a stick or a bat and live out the hopes and dreams he had held fast to.

He never forgot his upbringing. He knew that his mother worked hard to keep him in sports and other extracurricular activities. He was grateful that his grandfather had taken the time to drive him to and from practices for hockey and other sports. He didn't take these things for granted. He knew that not every young person was so fortunate. And he wanted very much to give back.

This led him to get involved with one of the charities that he is most known for helping, KidSport. Jarome says about KidSport: "This is a great group that assists financially challenged families with funding. When I was a kid these challenges were very real to me. KidSport is not just hockey either. I believe that all sports are great for kids." For every goal he scored, Jarome donated $1,000 to the Calgary chapter of KidSport. This was the start of Jarome's ongoing generosity.

In 2001, Jarome also played an essential role in helping the Flames Foundation. He was one of the main forces behind "The Puck in the Soup" dinner. At this event, Flames players waited on fans at a charity dinner. The money they raised went to help

From early on in his career, Jarome was a strong presence on the ice. Here he screens Toronto goalie Felix Potvin.

KidSport

KidSport is a Canadian children's charity that gives money to help children who might not otherwise be able to afford to get involved in sports. Their mission statement reads: *"We believe that no kid should be left on the sidelines and all should be given the opportunity to experience the positive benefits of organized sports. KidSport provides support to children in order to remove financial barriers that prevent them from playing organized sport."*

minor hockey programs and local hospitals, as well as various children's charities.

"The Puck in the Soup dinner, that was fun," Jarome said. "We waited on fans. Fans came out and bought tickets to the evening and it was a lot of fun. We had a little skit and that was an opportunity. As a team, we raised $100,000 so it felt good to be a part of that."

Goals for Cash

Jarome Iginla initially pledged $1,000 per goal to KidSport Calgary. In 2008 Jarome decided that he wasn't giving enough. He raised his donations to KidSport from $1,000 a goal to $2,000. In the 2008 All-Star Game he raised it even further: he gave the charity $5,000 for every goal scored.

Season	Goals scored	Donation
2000–01	31	$31,000
2001–02	52	$52,000
2002–03	35	$35,000
2003–04	41	$54,000
2005–06	35	$80,000
2006–07	39	$78,000
2007–08	50	$100,000
2008–09	35	$70,000
2009–10	32	$64,000

Jarome would also visit hospitals. He became part of the "Shoot for a Cure" program, designed to help find a cure for spinal cord injuries.

"We [the National Hockey League Players' Association] would love to see a cure for spinal cord injury and as hockey players, we know things can change any day," he said about the program.

It was quickly becoming obvious that Jarome was not only an important figure to Calgary hockey, but to the city and to children.

7 A Heart of Gold

By this time, people were starting to appreciate just what the Flames had in their pocket. Jarome was a quiet and reserved, yet determined, young man who was no longer an unknown player. He got better with each and every game. He was poised to be the Flames' rising star in the 2001–02 season.

What was sure to be a highlight of Jarome's career was representing his country in the 2002 Winter Olympics.

By the time the roster for the 2002 Winter Olympics was announced, Jarome was a great player, but he wasn't at superstar status. And Canada had its share of superstars. So Team Canada general manager Wayne Gretzky didn't call him in for the 2001 orientation camp. But Gretzky did add that players who showed their talent in the first half of the 2001–02 season would also be considered for a spot on the team.

Jarome got off to a fine start. By the end of the year, he led the league in scoring. With a bit of good luck for Jarome, and a bit of bad luck in the form of a shoulder injury for Team Canada's Simon Gagne, Jarome received the phone call he had hoped for. He was invited to the team's mini-camp in preparation for the Olympics. For three days, he played with the best of the best in Canadian hockey. But there was no guarantee that he would make the final cut.

After a short wait, Jarome found out. He had made it. Or had he? In a *Calgary Sun* article, he said, "I was really excited. I thought: 'That's awesome.' Then I thought: 'Ah, wait a minute here. It could be a joke. How embarrassing would it be to show up and not really be invited?'"

But it was no joke. "The Great One" himself, Wayne Gretzky, who held almost every NHL record imaginable, had called him the best forward in the league. Now, after representing his country at the World Juniors, and making it to the NHL, Jarome was on his way to representing his country in another worldwide event. And the event would propel him even further along to superstar status.

In September he joined other stars for the training camp. He trained alongside Brendan Shanahan, Martin Brodeur, Steve Yzerman, and Mario Lemieux. It was unlike anything he'd ever experienced.

"I don't think it was as much getting on the legs and going and skating at that speed before camp," he said. "I think it was more mental. You know, there were the best players, some of the best players in the game, and competing alongside of them and being part of it really helped my confidence."

When he arrived at the Olympics in Salt Lake City, Utah, he was slightly awestruck. He was playing with hockey's elite. He didn't play as hard as he normally did, taking a safer, more reserved style of play. After a 5–2 loss to Sweden in Game One, the pressure was on the Canadian team. Sure, it had only been one game, but it had been one game in *Canada's* game. They were expected to do better.

In the second game, against Germany, Jarome played on a line with Yzerman and Gagne, who had returned to the team. Team Canada won 3–2. The third game

Canada's rivals, the US men's hockey team, beneath the Olympic flame at the Opening Ceremonies.

was a 3–3 tie with the Czech Republic, a strong adversary.

When superstar Joe Sakic was moved from a line that included hockey icon Mario Lemieux to play with Jarome and Simon Gagne, Jarome got a boost of confidence.

In a *Sports Illustrated* article, he said, "Joe's like, 'Oh, it's going to be fun playing with you young guys.'" Iginla added, "A part of me was saying, He must be thinking, Why me? Going from Mario to us. But even if he felt it was a demotion, he never acted as if it was. That meant a lot."

Canada won the fourth game 2–1 and then rolled over Belarus 7–1 in the semifinal. Jarome scored the final goal.

The whole country was at a standstill during the gold-medal game against the United States. Russia may be Canada's top adversary in hockey, but the United States is the definite second.

The first period was intense. Just before it ended, Sakic ripped down the right wing. Jarome headed toward the net. An American defenseman was hot on his heels, but Jarome did what he did best: he kept on going with his eye on his final destination. Sakic fired off a shot and Jarome tipped the puck past goalie Mike Richter. Canada was a sea of cheers. It may have been a slim lead, but it was a lead nonetheless.

The Americans tied it up in the second, but then it was that line again: Sakic scored another goal. The clock was ticking. There was only one period left.

Canada managed to keep the Americans off the scoreboard for most of the period. But they hadn't managed a goal either. With such a slim lead, everyone was on the edge of their seats.

And then, there was that determined

young Jarome again. With just four minutes left in the period, he skated down the right wing straight for Richter. With the puck on his stick, he got in close, then fired off a shot that beat Richter. It was now 4–2 with fewer than four minutes left! And then Sakic scored another. The clock wound down and Canada captured

Jarome and his teammates Simon Gagne (left) and Joe Sakic (centre) with their gold medals from the 2002 Olympics.

the gold medal for the first time in 50 years. It was an experience Jarome would never forget.

Even in the high feelings of being part of a gold-medal game, part of a historic moment, the kind person that Jarome is shone through.

After the celebrations, Jarome went out to a local restaurant with his family. There, he met four college students who were fans. The men had travelled to Salt Lake City without tickets to the game. They didn't even have a place to stay. They had been sleeping in their car. Jarome spoke with them for a while and then politely excused himself. When he returned, he told the four shocked men that he had booked them into a hotel. And, of course, he had picked up the tab.

8 Breaking Barriers

At just twenty-four years old, Jarome had had a remarkable year. He was at the top of his game in the league and had been an important force in Canada's gold-medal win at the Winter Olympics. But, as important as hockey was to him, so was playing an important role in helping those less fortunate.

He once said, "As a child, sports had a positive influence on my life. No matter what a child's economic situation, I believe that everyone should have the opportunity to participate and experience the many benefits that sports can provide."

So he continued to take part in KidSport. "Part of the reason why I get involved in charity work is I feel very blessed and very fortunate to be in the NHL."

Seeing as he had scored 31 goals in 2000–01, his contribution of $1,000 per goal was a great boon to the organization. And he was also one of the most active participants from the Calgary Flames.

Jarome returned to Calgary to see if he could continue with his phenomenal season and maybe even improve upon his contributions to the charity.

When he returned to the NHL, he proved that he was one of the league's elite stars. On April 7, 2002, Jarome reached a milestone after he became the only NHL player to score 50 goals that season. In fact, he reached 52. He was only the second

NHL Foundation Charities

If you're an NHL player, your job doesn't just end on the ice. They also give back to the community. Many times they choose their own charities to contribute to, as Jarome has done. Not only do the players contribute themselves, but the teams also hold events to raise money. Sometimes they host dinner events, golf championships, or auctions. For Jarome, he's taken his good fortune to raise money for not just one charity, but for many. His hard work and dedication to helping those less fortunate earned him the NHL Player Foundation Award, an award that recognizes a player's commitment to charities in their community.

Calgary Flames player to do so, after Gary Roberts did it in 1992–93.

He won the Art Ross Trophy for most points scored in the regular season and the Maurice Richard Trophy for most goals scored in a season. This was a historic moment. He was the first black player ever to win the trophies.

"To be the first black player to win a scoring title is an honour," he said. "There will probably be other black players to win the scoring race, and when I have kids and grandkids, I'll be able to share my stories with them, even if they get sick of hearing them."

He also won the Lester B. Pearson Award for the "most outstanding player." Stars like Wayne Gretzky and Mario Lemieux had won this award. It was tremendous recognition for the hard work he had put in over the season. It was no wonder that he had been named assistant captain to the team — a sure sign that the Flames recognized his value. And Electronic Arts even named him as the featured player on the cover of their NHL 2003 game.

Jarome was helping break down the

Jarome was the first black player to win many NHL trophies. Here, he hoists the World Cup of Hockey Trophy that the Canadian team would win in 2004.

colour barrier in the NHL, which some people consider the "whitest" sport around. He was also a positive role model to children. He showed them that success didn't mean you thought only about yourself. He showed them what you could do for others with your success.

And Jarome wouldn't stop there, even if he faced struggles.

9 Captaincy

At the start of the 2002–03 season, Jarome said: "Trying to live up to expectation and being last year's scoring champ and scoring 50 goals again, those are the things I dreamed of when I was younger. I wanted to be a star player in the league. If you look at the elite players in the league, like Steve Yzerman and Joe Sakic and Brendan Shanahan, they face those pressures every night. Everyone tries to shut them down and tries to stop them, and they find ways to get it done." It was important for Jarome to make sure that *he* could get it done. But it was a tough challenge.

Although there were rumours of trading the Calgary superstar, "Iggy" signed a new two-year contract worth $13 million in September 2002. Both he and the Flames struggled at the start of the season. Jarome scored only four goals in 21 games. And then he was injured. At the beginning of December, he suffered a hip and groin injury. His chances of playing were judged day to day. Then almost two weeks later, he was out. He missed five games. He also suffered a hand injury after being in a fight.

Jarome managed to find his stride once again in the new year. He scored 35 goals, for 67 points by the end of the season. Even with his efforts, the Flames missed the playoffs for the seventh straight year. It was obvious that things weren't going to be easy. But Jarome took it with the grace and poise that he had become known for.

At this point, teammate Craig Conroy decided to step aside in his role as captain. He passed the "C" on to Jarome, the logical choice. Jarome was a natural leader. On the ice he was a fierce competitor, both offensively and defensively. He had great hands and possessed surprising speed. Even as a superstar, he wasn't afraid to drop the gloves if he needed to — although he was criticized by people who were afraid of him injuring himself. In interviews, he was polite and soft-spoken, with an infectious smile. He was involved in the community and it was important for him to help less fortunate children. And by this time, he had married his high-school sweetheart. All of this made him very likeable and what some would call a "hot commodity," meaning he was quite valuable.

So, after Conroy discussed the idea with coach Darryl Sutter, the captaincy was given to the Flames superstar. This was no ordinary captaincy. On October 8, 2003, Jarome became the NHL's first black captain. He was one of only thirteen blacks in the NHL at the time.

In a statement released after the announcement, Jarome said, "I have been very lucky to have played with many great captains that I have learned from over the course of my career . . . I'm ready for the next challenge and the responsibilities that go with it." There was no doubt that he could live up to the expectations.

Then, in February 2003, the trade rumours started swilling again. After a Flames scout was seen at a couple of New York Rangers games, people started whispering that Calgary was looking to dump the highly paid star.

Calgary's general manager, Craig

Button, denied the rumours. "There's no truth to it," he said in a New York newspaper article. "Definitely not. My interest is not to trade Jarome Iginla. My interest is to build with Jarome Iginla."

This would not be the last time trade rumours about Jarome popped up. As a superstar on a struggling team, it was bound to happen.

But he did remain with the team. And it was about to become one heck of a ride.

10 Cup-Bound

Jarome got his team off to a great start in the 2003–04 season. Perhaps it was his role as the team's new captain, or perhaps it was his drive to improve. Whatever it was, the Flames saw an improvement.

Backed by Flames goalie Miikka Kiprusoff, or "Kipper," the team seemed to be on a climb to the top.

By December, the team was on a streak. They had beaten Montreal and Toronto at a point in the season where they were usually on a downslide. These wins seemed to buoy the team. They went on to post a record of 13–3–3 by the start of the new year. The new year would prove to be a good one.

The team's success seemed to reflect Jarome's personal success — and he was having a great season. For the third time, Jarome was named to the All-Star team. By the end of the year, the young superstar had tallied 41 goals, tying with Rick Nash of the Columbus Blue Jackets and Ilya Kovalchuk of the Atlanta Thrashers for the Maurice Richard Trophy. The team's record was a stunning 92 points (42–30–7–3), their best in ten years. They made it to the playoffs for the first time in eight years — the last time was when Jarome had taken to the ice for his first NHL game.

With the team's success, the heat was on for them to advance. Every Canadian wanted to see a home team in the finals. But for Calgary and its young star, who had faced his own ups and downs, there was added pressure.

In the first round, the Flames defeated another Canadian team, the Vancouver Canucks. Their advance to the second round was a milestone: it was the first time they had won a playoff series since 1989. The team had won the Stanley Cup that year. Could this be a sign of good things to come?

In the second round, Calgary faced old-time playoff champs the Detroit Red Wings. In one game, Jarome even dropped the gloves with Derian Hatcher, a proven tough guy. The fact that their captain was ready to step up to one of the league's toughest players seemed to bolster the team. They went on to win the series in six games.

Next, the Flames faced the San Jose

Sharks. Kiprusoff had been acquired by the Flames from the Sharks. He wasn't worried about facing his old teammates. In fact, he played a key role in the series — along with star forward Jarome, of course.

The series was another hard-fought one. But the Flames prevailed once again in a nail-biting final. The Flames won the last game 3–1 after an empty-netter sealed the fate of the Sharks. Calgary was going on to the Stanley Cup finals! They became the first Canadian team to make it to the finals in ten years.

For Jarome, reaching the Stanley Cup finals was a dream come true. But the true dream would be to hoist the Cup. To do so meant playing his hardest and giving his all in every game. Jarome, as always, was prepared to do that.

The Flames faced the Tampa Bay Lightning in the finals. In the first game, Jarome played his hardest. He helped put his team ahead 2–0 when he scored on a breakaway. He continued to play hard.

"I thought [Jarome] had everything going; his feet going, he was driving to tough areas," coach Darryl Sutter said. "He was really good."

After losing the second game 4–1, the Flames — and Jarome — came out hard. As was typical, Jarome led by example. He scored and got an assist. But one of the most interesting events didn't involve a puck.

Vincent Lecavalier, Tampa's biggest and brightest star, shoved Jarome behind the net after Jarome checked him hard. Jarome was not about to be pushed around. He dropped the gloves. The two stars of their teams began a fight that landed Jarome in the penalty box. For much of the time that Jarome sat out, the fans chanted "Iggy."

Tampa Bay came back to win the fourth

game at just 1–0. The fifth game was an intense fight to the end. The series was tied and whoever won this game would lead the series 3–2, meaning, they could be the ones hoisting the coveted Cup after the very next game.

The game was fierce. Early in the second period, it was tied 1–1. But Jarome would have none of that. At one point, he blasted down the wing with the puck and blew a shot that bounced off the post and past Tampa goalie Nikolai Khabibulin.

Tampa wasn't ready to roll over just yet. In the third, they managed to tie it up. Once again, it was captain Jarome to the rescue. He had what some call the best shift of his career. He was targeted by Tampa players — rightfully so, as he was an obvious threat — and even lost his helmet at one point. But he wouldn't be stopped. He skated out in front of the Tampa Bay net, facing centre ice, and then spun, taking a shot on net. The puck hit Khabibulin. But teammate Oleg Saprykin took the puck — and scored!

The Flames were heading home for Game Six, with the chance to win the Cup in front of a home crowd. It was sure to be an intense game. Even more than Game Five had been.

Sure enough, the sixth game was a nail-biter. The score was tight. The Lightning scored first, but the Flames quickly followed. The second period was the same: Tampa scored, followed by Calgary. In the third period, the Flames played hard and even dominated. But the period remained scoreless. The teams went into double overtime before Tampa Bay's Martin St. Louis scored. The dream of winning at home was gone.

Jarome had said that he didn't feel that he'd played his best that night. But he was ready for the game of his life: Game Seven in the Stanley Cup finals.

But the game didn't go as he planned.

Tampa Bay came out at the Flames hard. By the second period, they were leading 2–1. The Flames just couldn't get one in the net. Not even to tie it up. The dream of drinking from the Cup would have to wait. Although it had been quite a year for Jarome — becoming captain at the beginning of the year and reaching the Stanley Cup finals — his final prize eluded him.

11 Life after the Finals

In 2004, *The Hockey News* called Jarome the best player in the league. There were many who agreed. And he was awarded the NHL Foundation Award for Community Service as well as the King Clancy Memorial Trophy in recognition of his contributions to charitable organizations.

After such a fantastic ride, what awaited Jarome for the 2004–05 season?

As it turned out, not much.

The NHL couldn't reach an agreement

with its players over salaries. So the league and its owners locked out the players. This meant that they couldn't play any games. As the year went on, it was clear that no agreement would be reached. On February 16, 2005, the NHL cancelled what would have been its eighty-eighth season. It was the first time that the Stanley Cup would not be played for since 1919.

Many NHL players wanted to continue making money or stay in shape and be ready for the next season. Some played elsewhere, many in Europe and Russia.

What did Jarome do? He decided to remain at home and stay in shape.

In a *Sports Illustrated* article, Jarome talked about hockey. "Sometimes you get an opportunity in the first 10 seconds," he said. "But it could come at the end of your shift. If you're tired, you might miss your chance." That's why he spent the next year working out. He worked on building up his speed and endurance.

But thinking about himself wasn't what Jarome was all about. His mind was always on charity. He wanted to promote hockey to those less fortunate, or those less likely to try to play it professionally.

In November 2004, Jarome joined NHLers Anson Carter, Donald Brashear, Fred Brathwaite, and — his hero and Hall of Famer — Grant Fuhr to take part in a hockey clinic in a suburb near Chicago, Illinois. The clinic was designed to interest young, inner-city, minority children in the game of hockey. On hand was the man who is considered to have broken the colour barrier back in the 1950s, Willie O'Ree.

"We in the National Hockey League believe that hockey is a sport for everyone," said O'Ree. "We want to get rid of the notion that hockey is an all-white sport, played by only white players."

Willie O'Ree was the first black player to appear in an NHL game. He played for the Boston Bruins in a game at the Montreal Forum on January 18, 1958.

It was a feeling many of these professional black NHL players shared. And it was particularly important at a time when there were fewer than fifteen black players in the entire league.

That year Jarome also played in the World Cup of Hockey with stars like Joe Sakic and Mario Lemieux. Obviously, it was yet another great honour. But what Jarome wanted, as most players did, was to get back to the NHL.

12 Back to Work

In July 2005, the players and owners reached an agreement. It was a relief to both hockey players and fans alike. The players wanted to get back to doing what they loved. The fans wanted to cheer on their favourite players and teams.

Jarome welcomed the return to the NHL as well. He could finally get back to doing what he loved most: hitting the ice and fighting hard for a win. But the 2005–06 season wouldn't be quite as

The NHL's New Rules

• Zero tolerance on interference, hooking, and holding/obstruction.

• A player who instigates a fight in the final five minutes of a game will receive a game misconduct and an automatic one-game suspension. The length of suspension doubles for each additional incident.

• In addition to the minor penalty for unsportsmanlike conduct/diving that may be assessed by the referee during a game, Hockey Operations will review game videos and assess fines to players who dive or embellish a fall or a reaction, or who feign injury in an attempt to draw penalties.

• The first such incident will result in a warning letter being sent to the player.

• The second such incident will result in a $1,000 fine.

• The third such incident will result in a $2,000 fine.

• The fourth such incident will result in a one-game suspension.

rewarding as his previous season.

The team started off poorly. They were a miserable 4–7–2. Then, in November, they hit a winning streak. Things were looking good. But by the beginning of December, Jarome had hit a scoring drought. He had gone nine games without a goal. It wasn't hard to imagine how incredibly frustrating this was for a star player like Jarome. Had the lockout made him lose his touch?

During the lockout, new rules had come into play that were supposed to make the NHL "cleaner." For years, players had dropped the gloves ready for fights. Each team had a "goon:" a designated player who would protect star players or who would stir things up. This was changed. There were stricter rules about fighting. Now there would be more of a focus on the actual game and skills required to put the puck in the net. This was all good news for stars like Jarome.

Finally, on December 7, Jarome scored. Then the team picked up speed, and seemed sure to make the playoffs again. Not only did they make the playoffs, they also finished at the top of their division. They finished eight points ahead of the Edmonton Oilers and Colorado Avalanche, who each had 95 points.

Headed to the playoffs, there was great hope. Fans were eager to see their team in the finals. But there were doubts. Did the team have what it would take to make it to the finals for the second time in a row? Or were they working hard with just two star players: Jarome and Kipper? The team was definitely talented, but many times, when a game was lost, or when they would go on a losing streak, all fingers would point to Jarome. He was excellent captain material: he would readily take the blame for a bad game played. But it wasn't fair to expect so much with just one star forward.

Sure enough, the Flames showed that they were lacking in depth. They had excellent goaltending and a superstar forward, but not much of anything else. They had young guys like Dion Phaneuf on defense. He was a talented player, but he lacked what the team needed.

In the first round, the Flames were eliminated by the Mighty Ducks of Anaheim in seven games. The Flames and their fans were disappointed. But perhaps no one was more disappointed than Jarome.

The 2006–07 season got off to a horrible start for the Calgary Flames. On the road, the team was 3–7–3. But, on the up side, they seemed unbeatable at home. In less than a month, the team won eight games in a row at the Calgary Saddledome.

Then, on December 7, 2006, Jarome set his own personal best by scoring his

300th career goal and 600th career point. It was quite the milestone for Jarome. Yet, despite his rise to NHL stardom, he hadn't lost his sense of humility.

"The thing with Iggy is that he doesn't ever talk about himself at all," said teammate Craig Conroy. "On the ice he's full of confidence. But he'll never let you know about it. It's not his personality."

13 Olympic Fever

When the Winter Olympics came around again in 2006, Jarome was given another shot at representing his country on the world stage. Not only was he named to the team, he was also named an alternate captain — another great honour.

There was a lot of pressure on Team Canada going into the Olympics in Turin, Italy. After all, the team of all-star players had brought home a gold medal after a fifty-year drought in men's hockey. Once again, Gretzky was the coach, and he put together what many thought was an invincible team. Canadians hoped that their team could prove that Canada was home to hockey.

But Canada struggled. It wasn't the fierce battle on the ice that many fans had hoped for or expected. Instead, Canada lost game after game. Then they lost the quarter-final, and finally finished seventh overall. Canadians were stunned and severely disappointed. Many fans raised questions about the players, the roster, and the coaching. It was Gretzky who stepped up and took the blame.

"Quite honestly, I'm going to re-assess where I fit and what I'm going to do in the future," said Gretzky after the game. "Hockey Canada is wonderful, my country is great, and I love it dearly. But I'm also human, too. It's tough and it's nerve-wracking. It's not fun when you don't win."

Despite the disappointing finish at the Olympics, Jarome returned home to Calgary still very much a star. That season, he played in all 82 games. He finished the season with 35 goals and 32 assists for 67 points. Although it was nowhere near the 50-goal season he had in 2002, there were many people who felt that this wasn't necessarily a reflection on him, but on the team as a whole.

That season, the Flames finished with 103 points. They were at the top of their division, but were eliminated in the first round, in seven games by the Anaheim Ducks (formerly the Mighty Ducks of Anaheim).

The following season, in 2006–07, the team finished with 96 points, squeaking into the playoffs. And, once again, they were eliminated in the first round by the Detroit Red Wings. It was clear that there was still some work to be done.

Jarome needed to have someone who could support him on the ice. Sure, they had young promising players like defenseman Dion Phaneuf, but clearly, it wasn't enough.

The next few seasons were disappointing for the team. Coaching changes didn't seem to help. In 2007–08, the Flames were eliminated in the first round and, again, the next season as well. Yet, each season, there was Jarome, on the ice, giving it his all. In every season, he led all players in points and scoring.

The 2010 Olympics changed everything. Thirty-two-year-old Jarome was heading into his third Winter Games. He had been fortunate enough to win gold in 2002, but missed out in 2006. What would 2010 bring?

This time it was Steve Yzerman, former Detroit Red Wings superstar, who was putting together the Canadian team.

Still a Winner

Jarome's awards, trophies, and medals:

2010 Olympic Gold Medal

2008–09 Mark Messier Leadership Award

2003–04 Maurice Richard Trophy (for most goals)

2003–04 King Clancy Memorial Trophy (Humanitarian of the Year)

2002 Olympic Gold Medal

2001–02 Lester B. Pearson Award (Player of the Year selected by the NHLPA)

2001–02 Art Ross Trophy (Leading Scorer)

2001–02 Maurice Richard Trophy

2001–02 NHL First All-Star Team

Jarome was honoured with the chance to represent his country again. But this time, it was a chance in a lifetime — the opportunity to represent his country *in* his country. The 2010 Winter Olympics would be played in Vancouver, British Columbia. Not only were fans pumped, but so were the stars of the team.

Team Canada was replete with superstars: Sidney Crosby, Roberto Luongo, and Martin Brodeur, just to name a few. Jarome was one of many.

The series started off well enough. Jarome got the first hat trick of the series (his third goal was first credited to teammate Rick Nash). But then things started to take a turn for the worse when Team Canada went down to the United States. It was a crushing defeat. Most fans thought that Canada would be eliminated from even a bronze-medal finish. But they weren't out yet.

It seemed like an impossible feat: defeat Germany, Slovakia, and Russia to make it to the gold medal game. But they did it.

And guess who they had to face in the final? The United States!

Having lost to them in the round robin, it was a perfect gold-medal faceoff.

Ryan Miller, the American goalie, was

phenomenal. Team Canada had difficulty getting the puck past him. By the third period, Canada was holding on to a 2–1 lead. But then, in the final minute of the third period, the incredible happened: the United States managed to tie it up. Screams of disappointment could be heard around the country.

When the overtime period started, Canadians were on the edge of their seats. To lose in such a close game, and at home, would be crushing.

It was 7:40 into the overtime period. Sidney Crosby passed the puck to Jarome deep into the US zone. Ryan Suter was close on Jarome while Crosby drove to the net. All Jarome heard was "Iggy!" Falling as he did, Jarome passed the puck to the voice. The next thing he knew, the home crowd was on its feet — as was all of Canada.

"I'd fallen down so I didn't see it go in

The Greatest Goals

Sidney Crosby's gold-medal winning goal at the 2010 Olympics will go down in history as one of Canada's most important hockey moments. For many hockey fans, it is as important as the goal scored by Paul Henderson in the 1972 Summit Series. The Summit Series was a meeting of Canada's best NHL players against the Soviet Union's best. Canadians thought that the Soviets would be no match for their NHL stars. However, the Canadians were surprised by the Soviets' skill, and they almost lost the series. It came down to the final game in the Soviet Union. Canadians at home stopped what they were doing to watch the game: schools pulled out television sets; people stayed home from work to watch the dramatic game. Amazingly, Canada tied it up in the third period to make it 5–5. With just seconds left, Paul Henderson picked up a rebound of the Soviets' goalie and won the game. Canadians erupted in cheers and went out into the streets celebrating. It has long been considered one of Canada's most memorable hockey moments.

or anything but the crowd, him [Crosby] jumping around was one of the better feelings. The excitement . . . to win in overtime. Those are what you dream of when you're a young kid, to be part of a team to win in overtime, jumping off the bench, throwing your sticks and all that stuff. It was pretty wild," he said of the win.

Later, Sidney Crosby would say that he didn't even see the puck go in the net. He and Jarome were two players who just acted on instinct.

"I'm very proud to be Canadian," Jarome said after the historic win. "You know what, I'm really proud of setting the gold-medal record for Canada."

When Jarome returned to the Flames, everyone expected to see his gold medal around his neck. But it was nowhere to be seen.

"I think my daughter took it to school, actually. To kindergarten, so it's my wife's responsibility today," he said.

Sure enough, his five-year-old daughter had brought his medal to kindergarten.

With this act, Jarome had once again proven that he always gives his all — to himself, his fans, and to those who need him most: children.

Epilogue

Jarome Iginla is a player with many faces: the hard worker, the leader, the smiling superstar, the giver, and the role model. And he wears these faces with ease. He is a genuinely kind person always aiming to improve and to try to make the lives of others better.

Some criticize him for not being constant. But he *is* constant. He always seeks to better himself.

In a statement released by KidSport,

Diane Jones Konihowski, KidSport Alberta's chair said, "Jarome has been such a tremendous supporter of both KidSport Calgary and KidSport Canada for the past nine seasons and the humility and graciousness with which he's supported the charitable organization over the years is a testament to his true character . . . Thank you, Jarome, you've helped over 2,500 kids and have inspired many more."

And he's always hoping to be a role model to young black children who might love the game of hockey, but think that they don't stand a chance.

He once told ESPN.com, "I hope more black kids get involved in hockey. It's an awesome sport, and hopefully, it's a positive."

In 2009 Jarome won the Mark Messier Leadership Award. This is an award given by the NHL recognizing superior leadership within hockey and as a contributing member of society. It only makes sense: since 2000, Jarome has been an ambassador for KidSport Calgary. He also supports the Juvenile Diabetes Research Foundation and Doctors Without Borders. Plus he is a member of the Garth Brooks Teammates for Kids Foundation. Jarome has donated a lot of his time and his money to many various causes. He supports literacy programs and youth hockey programs as well as hockey diversity initiatives.

Jarome's intensity on and off the ice is sure to be felt for years to come. He is a determined man: whether it's determination to play hard and his best or to make the lives of children better.

As a player, he is the ultimate captain. He is a leader. He takes responsibility for failures and isn't one to boast about successes. He isn't afraid to stand up for what is right, even if it means getting into a fight once in a while. And he is always humble.

"He's grounded," Flames general manager Craig Button once said. "He doesn't carry himself with any attitude or arrogance. He's confident in his abilities. He's self-assured. He's genuine. He's a better person than he is a player, and we all know what kind of player he is."

Great words about a great player — and a great person.

Glossary

Centre: Forward position on a hockey team that plays between the right wing and left wing positions.

Centre ice: The area between the two blue lines on a hockey rink; also called the "neutral zone."

(NHL Entry) Draft: A yearly event where rights to unsigned players are spread out among NHL teams.

Overtime: An additional period added to break a tie in a hockey game; in a regular season game, the overtime period is five minutes.

Period: A twenty-minute period of time during which teams play; in hockey, there are three periods, with a fifteen-minute break in play (called an intermission) between each.

Playoff: A tournament played by teams to determine a champion within a league.

Right wing: A forward position on a hockey team that plays right of centre.

Underage player: A player who does not fall within the normal age range in a particular league.

Upstart: A person who has risen to fame.

Wins, Losses, Overtime losses: In the NHL, each team posts their statistics from games played throughout the year. Teams are awarded two points for a win, no points for a loss, and one point for an overtime loss. If a team has played a season with a record of 30–38–14, that means the team has won 30 games, lost 38, and gone into overtime 14 times. This would give them 74 points for the season.

About the Author

Nicole Mortillaro is a veteran children's sports books editor. She is the author of the Recordbook *Something to Prove: The story of hockey tough guy Bobby Clarke.* She has also written books on weather for children, and astronomy for adults. Nicole is a first-generation Canadian born to a Guyanese mother and an Italian father. She now lives north of Toronto with her daughter.

Photo Credits

We gratefully acknowledge the following sources for permission to reproduce the images in this book.

Hockey Hall of Fame: front cover (top); back cover (middle); back cover (top) and p 19; p 28 (Doug MacLellan/Hockey Hall of Fame); p 35 (Lanny Church/Hockey Hall of Fame); p 38, p 48 (David Klutho/Hockey Hall of Fame); p 59 (Dave Sandford/HHOF-IIHF Images); cover, back cover (bottom) and p 65 (Matthew Manor/Hockey Hall of Fame); p 83 (James McCarthy/Hockey Hall of Fame).

Index

More gripping underdog tales of sheer determination and talent!

○ RECORDBOOKS

Recordbooks are action-packed true stories of Canadian athletes who have changed the face of sport. Check out these titles available at bookstores or your local library, or order them online at www.lorimer.ca.

Big League Dreams: Baseball Hall of Fame's first African-Canadian, Fergie Jenkins by Richard Brignall

Choice of Colours: The pioneering African-American quarterbacks who changed the face of football by John Danakas

Fighting for Gold: The story of Canada's sledge hockey Paralympic gold by Lorna Schultz Nicholson

Jordon Tootoo: The highs and lows in the journey of the first Inuit to play in the NHL by Melanie Florence

Long Shot: How the Winnipeg Falcons won the first Olympic hockey gold by Eric Zweig

Pink Power: The first Women's World Hockey Champions by Lorna Schultz Nicholson

Something to Prove: The story of hockey tough guy Bobby Clarke by Nicole Mortillaro

Small Town Glory: The story of the Kenora Thistles' remarkable quest for the Stanley Cup by John Danakas and Richard Brignall

Star Power: The legend and lore of Cyclone Taylor by Eric Zweig

Tough Guys: Hockey rivals in times of war and disaster by Eric Zweig

Winning Gold: Canada's incredible 2002 Olympic victory in women's hockey by Lorna Schultz Nicholson